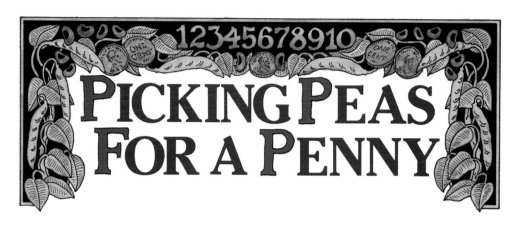

PICKING PEAS FOR A PENNY

Flynn

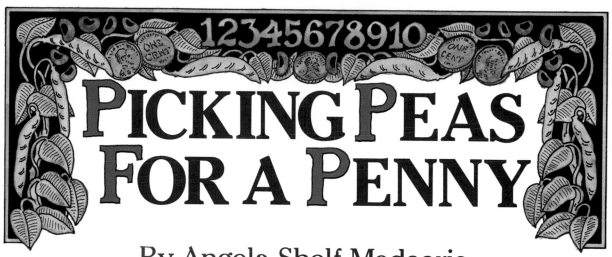

PICKING PEAS FOR A PENNY

By Angela Shelf Medearis
Drawings by Charles Shaw

SCHOLASTIC INC.

New York Toronto London Auckland Sydney

ISBN 0-590-45942-2

Copyright © 1990 by State House Press.
All rights reserved. Published by Scholastic Inc.,
730 Broadway, New York, NY 10003, by arrangement with
State House Press.
BLUE RIBBON is a registered trademark of Scholastic Inc.

12 11 10 9 8 7 6 5 4 3 2   4 5 6 7 8/9

Printed in the U.S.A.   23
First Scholastic printing, April 1993

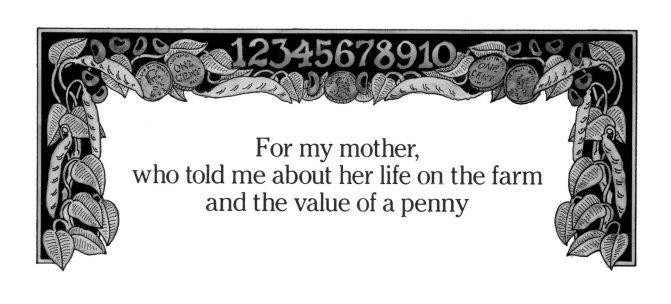

For my mother,
who told me about her life on the farm
and the value of a penny

Let me tell you a story that my mama told me about picking peas in the 1930s.

Now times were hard, and times were tough,
so picking peas for a living was plenty good enough.

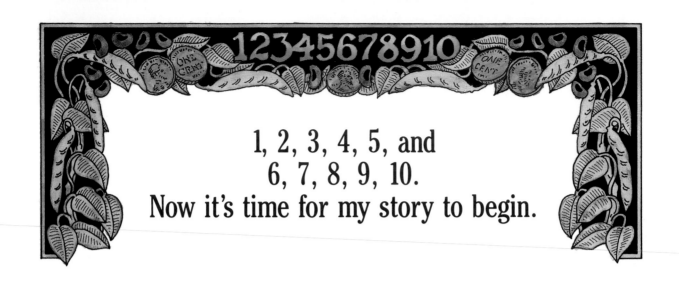

1, 2, 3, 4, 5, and
6, 7, 8, 9, 10.
Now it's time for my story to begin.

Picking peas for a penny
plenty work to be done,
in a field full of peas
under the morning sun.

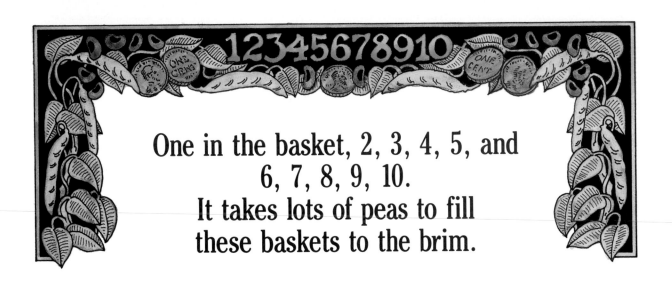

One in the basket, 2, 3, 4, 5, and
6, 7, 8, 9, 10.
It takes lots of peas to fill
these baskets to the brim.

We pick those peas under the hot morning sun.
We work a while, then we have some fun.
Then Grandma hollers out, "Get back to work
or you'll never get done!"

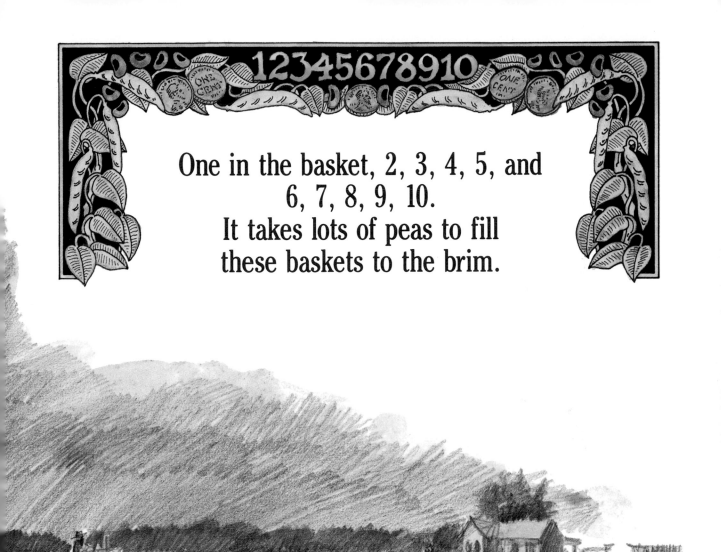

One in the basket, 2, 3, 4, 5, and
6, 7, 8, 9, 10.
It takes lots of peas to fill
these baskets to the brim.

Now the sun is straight up in the sky,
and it's as hot as hot can be.
We sure are glad when it's time to eat lunch
because it must be 100 degrees.

We eat and drink and eat and then,
it's time to start picking those peas again.

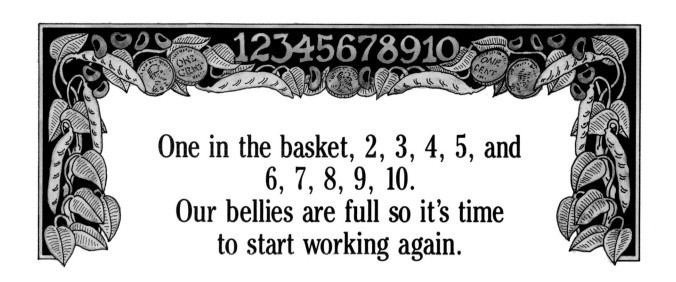

One in the basket, 2, 3, 4, 5, and
6, 7, 8, 9, 10.
Our bellies are full so it's time
to start working again.

Grandpa promises us a penny a pound,
and maybe even a trip into town,
if we can pick all these peas before the sun goes down.
We start working harder. We pick up the pace.
My brother and I have a pea-picking race.

Ten 10's make 100, and 100 pennies make one dollar, when we finish working I'm going to jump and shout and holler.

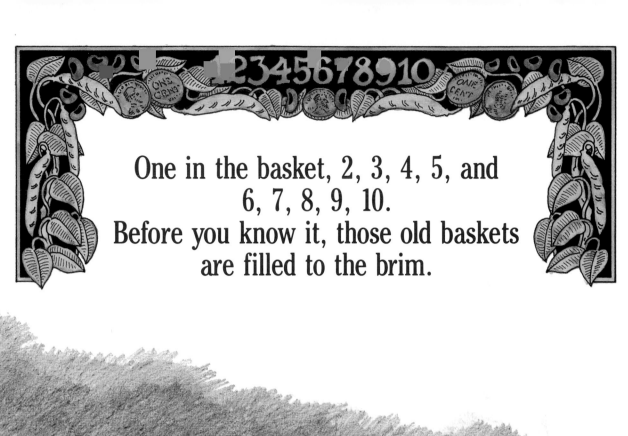

One in the basket, 2, 3, 4, 5, and
6, 7, 8, 9, 10.
Before you know it, those old baskets
are filled to the brim.

Now we're all smiles because the hard work is done.
We're going to go to town to have us some fun.
My brother and I giggle, and laugh, and grin.
We're through picking peas, now the fun can begin!

We climb into the wagon feeling mighty fine.
The whole day is before us, the hard work far behind.

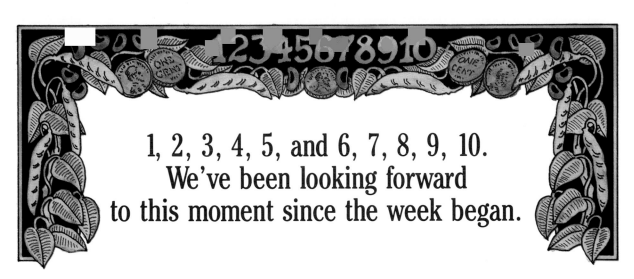

1, 2, 3, 4, 5, and 6, 7, 8, 9, 10.
We've been looking forward
to this moment since the week began.

Our pockets make tinkly music when we walk into the store.
We jingle, jangle, jingle across the wooden floor.

We look at all the pretty things and peer into each bin.
We're feeling mighty good 'cause we have money to spend.

Picking peas for a penny
is mighty hard work to do;
but those bright, shiny pennies
look mighty good when the work is through.

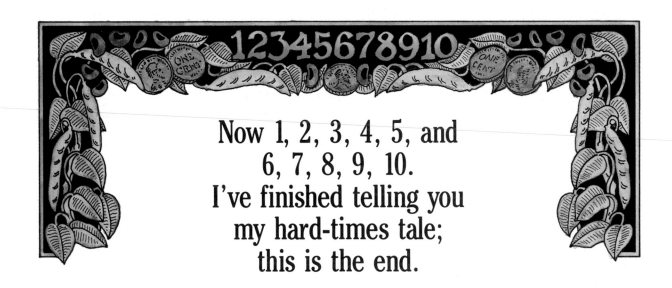

Now 1, 2, 3, 4, 5, and
6, 7, 8, 9, 10.
I've finished telling you
my hard-times tale;
this is the end.

The Davis Family. *(front, left to right)* Tom, Liz, Leon, Icie, Ricky; *(back, left to right)* Florine, John, Willie Mae, Leo, Angeline, and Imogene.

Picking Peas for a Penny is a rhythmical, richly lyrical counting rhyme and a biographical poem filled with heartwarming memories about the author's mother Angeline, her uncle John, and life on their grandparents' farm during the Depression.

About the Author

Angela Shelf Medearis is Director of *Book Boosters,* a reading motivation and literacy program for elementary school children. She has received numerous grants in support of her work as a literacy tutor. Mrs. Medearis resides in Austin, Texas, with her husband Michael, her daughter D.D., and several stacks of children's books.

About the Illustrator

Artist Charles Shaw's beautifully executed drawings are featured in hundreds of books for children and adults, including *Little Johnny Raindrop,* James Michener's *Texas,* and *Indian Life in Texas.* His paintings can be found in galleries, banks, and museums throughout the United States. Mr. Shaw resides in Dripping Springs, Texas, with his wife and three children.